T0130131

Conversations With Jesus

Fear
2
Peace

Barbara Baker

BALBOA.
PRESS
A DIVISION OF HAY HOUSE

Balboa Press books may be ordered through booksellers or by contacting:

Balboa Press
A Division of Hay House
1663 Liberty Drive
Bloomington, IN 47403
www.balboapress.com
1 (877) 407-4847

Because of the dynamic nature of the Internet, any web addresses or links contained in this book may have changed since publication and may no longer be valid. The views expressed in this work are solely those of the author and do not necessarily reflect the views of the publisher, and the publisher hereby disclaims any responsibility for them.

The author of this book does not dispense medical advice or prescribe the use of any technique as a form of treatment for physical, emotional, or medical problems without the advice of a physician, either directly or indirectly. The intent of the author is only to offer information of a general nature to help you in your quest for emotional and spiritual well-being. In the event you use any of the information in this book for yourself, which is your constitutional right, the author and the publisher assume no responsibility for your actions.

Any people depicted in stock imagery provided by Thinkstock are models, and such images are being used for illustrative purposes only. Certain stock imagery © Thinkstock.

Print information available on the last page.

ISBN: 978-1-5043-8676-0 (sc)
ISBN: 978-1-5043-8678-4 (hc)
ISBN: 978-1-5043-8677-7 (e)

Library of Congress Control Number: 2017913536

Balboa Press rev. date: 08/29/2017

Table of Contents

This project is dedicated in loving
memory of Bill Sturm.

Addictions

My dear child, I see you struggling with your addiction feeling defeated by it. Remember, when I walked this Earth many years ago I was tempted too, so I understand your pain and I will help you through your struggle. It may seem to you that this is too much to handle. This addiction has become a part of your life. But remember, My child, NOTHING is impossible with Me by your side. I am much bigger than your addiction.

Take one day at a time and ask for My guidance and I will give you enough grace for the day as I promise in Matthew 6:34 -- *"So do not worry about tomorrow; for tomorrow will care for itself"* *(Matthew 6:34, NASB).* Each day has enough trouble of its own. Read My Bible daily and ask The Holy Spirit to help you to understand it. My Word has the solutions to all of life's troubles. You have no control over your future, but I do. So give it to Me and take one day at a time and you will be amazed at what I will do in your life!

The pleasures I gave you in this world were meant for your temporary enjoyment, not to enslave you. An activity may start out as fun but when it becomes an addiction, and all you think about, it is time to give it to Me and I will turn your pain to purpose. I never waste pain.

There are many reasons for addictions: genetics, mental illness, peer pressure, loneliness, stress, escape from current life situations, or simply boredom. There are verses in The Bible to help with all of these. You live in a fallen world where the temptations of the devil are very real and can be overcome by prayer.

Take comfort, My child as the Bible states *"No temptation has overtaken you that is not common to man. I am faithful, and I will not let you be tempted beyond your ability, but with the temptation I will also provide the way of escape, that you may be able to endure it" (1 Corinthians 10:13, ESV).*

Look for signs that I am giving you to help you. I may send a friend to help, I may lead you to do some work for Me like helping others with their addictions. Trust in Me and I will show you a way out. Stay away from bad company who will influence you to stray. Change your environment. Ask Me to change your desires. I love to grant you anything that will bring you closer to Me!

Turning to Me in prayer will always be the better choice.

It took some time for this to become an addiction so at times you may find yourself giving in to these temptations, so do not beat yourself up! You are human and surrendering yourself to Me is a life-long process so do not give up. Repent and come back to Me. I will be waiting for you with open arms as I am a loving and forgiving God.

As I said I will never waste pain so I may ask you to help others with the same addiction as they will listen to one who has walked in their shoes. If you want to find true happiness, look for ways to be a blessing to others. You were made by Me and for Me so by looking for ways to help others you will experience the kind of joy only I can give.

Addictions lead to feelings of guilt, shame, hopelessness, despair, failure, rejection, and anxiety. These are the work of the devil. You will find in Me the Fruits of The Holy Spirit which are: charity, joy, peace, patience, kindness, goodness, generosity, gentleness, faithfulness, modesty and self-control. So seek Me and you will experience these gifts to the fullest. Remember to take it one day at a time because I will give you enough Grace just for the day. I am the God of yesterday, today, and tomorrow so do not worry about the future for I am already there. I love you My child and will never leave you to handle this alone!

Anger

My precious child, I see you with so much anger inside. This saddens Me as I am in you and I am love. Anger can be one of the most intense, destructive, and unhealthy emotions that you can experience. If not handled in the proper way, you can have drastic life-changing consequences.

This is why I left you with My Word, The Bible, which was meant to be your guide through life. I also left you with My gift of The Holy Spirit, who will help you to understand My Word. All you have to do is ask Him.

First, give your anger to Me and I will calm your heart as I promised in The Bible – *"My dear brothers and sisters, take note of this: Everyone should be quick to listen, slow to speak and slow to become angry, because human anger does not produce the righteousness that God desires" (James 1:19-20, NIV).*

When you take the time before reacting to a situation and pray to Me for guidance, I will bring your heart the peace only I can provide. You will then be able to move forward and resolve the problem with a calm heart which will produce the best outcome for all. Trust Me, you will be amazed how quick I work in you!

Anger is a secondary emotion. Ask Me to reveal the real reason for your anger. I will help you discover what it is you need to work on to resolve the real problem. Most anger comes from the feeling of not being in total control of your life. Trust in Me, surrender control to Me, and watch what wonderful things I will do in your life! I make this promise to you in Jeremiah 29:11 – *"For I know the plans I have for you," declares the LORD "plans to prosper you and not to harm you, plans to give you hope and a future" (Jeremiah 29:11, NIV).*

Anger is also a response to the feeling of being overwhelmed or exhausted. When I walked this Earth many years ago I took much needed time just to be quiet, sit, and pray. The world tells you that you must constantly be doing something in order to be productive. You set goals and strive very hard to accomplish them. Although goal setting is important, learning to enjoy the journey of getting to your goals is even more important. Talk to Me about your goals and I will make your path straight. I will teach you how to enjoy the moment and to live in the present. This will calm your spirit and remove your anger. When life gets to be overwhelming do what I did many years ago, take the time to sit and pray. This way you will move forward with peace.

Anger can also come from being treated unfairly or from what someone did to you. When you stay connected to Me you will not be concerned about the actions of others. Find comfort in Psalm 37:7-8 – *"Be still before the LORD and wait patiently for him; do not fret when people succeed in their ways, when they carry out their wicked schemes. Refrain from anger and turn from wrath; do not fret- it leads only to evil"* (Pslam 37:7-8, NIV).

Get up every day and ask Me how you can be a blessing to others. I will then work in you to change you from the inside out. This will be pleasing to Me and you will find great joy and happiness. I created everything for your joy and pleasure, but most days you do not even notice My works. The beautiful sunrise that you woke up to this morning, the gentle breeze that I kiss you with, the colorful flowers everywhere, and the birds of the air flying with no care.

I want you to have a full and abundant life My child. This anger can steal the joy I have planned for you if you are not careful. My gift to you is life itself, your gift to Me is what you do with it. Life will not always be easy for you, it was never meant to be, but together we can get through any problems. Find comfort in John 16:33 -- *"I have told you these things, so that in Me you may have peace. In this world you will have trouble. But take heart! I have overcome the world"* (John 16:33, NIV).

So, My precious child, the next time you feel anger building up inside of you simply call My name and I will come to you. I will turn your anger into something good. When you seek Me with your whole heart and love Me above anything or anyone else, there will be no room for anger in your heart, only love. I love you My dear child and I will never leave you alone.

Anxiety/Worry

My dear child, I see you worried about many things that you do not have total control over.

First of all, remember and take comfort in the fact that I did not create you just to leave you on your own. Those thoughts you have: fear of something happening, fear of you going crazy, feeling out of control - these thoughts can really take over your life if you let them. Replace these thoughts with My promises and make your faith bigger than your fear!

The biggest message I give in My Word, the Bible is "do not be afraid." When you have these scary thoughts, surrender them to Me and I will turn them to good if you truly trust Me. I gave you My word, The Bible, to be your compass in life. If you give power to a single negative thought then you are in danger of those thoughts giving life to fear, judgement, anger, and obsession.

Most fear comes from attachment to someone or something. Do not be attached to anything in this world for you were created to live in eternity with Me. Be comforted, My child, by My promise in 2 Corinthians 4:18 – *"So we don't look at the troubles we can see now; rather, we fix our gaze on things that cannot be seen. For the things we see now will soon be gone, but the things we cannot see will last forever" (2 Corinthians 4:18, NLT)*.

That is true with fear too. If you do not dwell on scary thoughts, rather dwell on My promises you will see fear disappear. You fill your mind with so many 'what ifs' that never happen. Worry means you do not trust Me. It cannot change the past or control the future, it just messes up today.

When I left this world many years ago I gave you the gift of The Holy Spirit who dwells in you to be your guide through life as promised in John 14:27 - *"I am leaving you with a gift – peace of mind and heart. And the peace I give is a gift the world cannot give. So don't be troubled or afraid" (John 14:27, NLT)*. When your mind wanders to scary thoughts say this verse over and over and really let it sink in. You will experience REAL peace that only I can give.

I hear your prayers My dear child and I have great plans for your life which you will find in Jeremiah 29:11 -- *"For I know the plans I have for you,"* declares the LORD, *"plans to prosper you and not to harm you, plans to give you hope and a future"* *(Jeremiah 29:11, NIV)*. This world tells you it is a sign of weakness to constantly need Me. This is simply not true, for I created you to need Me. The world says 'be strong' I say, "Let Me be your strength."

My promise states in Romans 12:2 – *"Do not conform to the pattern of this world, but be transformed by the renewing of your mind. Then you will be able to test and approve what God's will is—his good, pleasing and perfect will"* *(Romans 12:2, NIV)*. So turn off those anxious thoughts and replace them with thankful praise and watch what I do in your life! You will be amazed. Take everyday life, your eating, sleeping, working, your plans for fun, everything you do and place it before Me as an offering. Embracing what I have done for you is pleasing to Me. I love a trusting thankful heart.

You have trained your mind to worry so now it is time to train your mind to trust. This will take time but I will hold your hand every step of the way! So If you want to experience My peace do the following: worry about nothing, pray about everything, thank Me in all things, keep your mind on good things and be content in all things.

So as you see My child there is a way to calm your anxious mind. The mind is a wonderful gift I gave you but if you fill it with too much noise it will be hard to hear Me. Keep Me close and read My promises to you. Getting to know Me in a deep personal way will help you through the most difficult challenges of your life. Do not look for Me outside of yourself for I am in you.

Take one day at a time, surrender your fears to Me, realize that most of what you fear I would never allow to happen. Rest in Me and I will bring you peace. I love you My child and would NEVER leave you to face your fears alone.

Belief

My dear child, I see you struggling with belief in Me. You are experiencing many painful things that make you question if I am real. You live in a fallen world in which evil is very much a part of. When I gave you free will, as I wanted you to love Me freely, many people turned from Me and sin entered the world.

When I walked this Earth many years ago, I suffered a horrible death on the cross so that you may live in eternity with Me in Heaven. To get there you must believe in Me as your personal savior. I love you so much and want you to live with Me in Heaven, that I left you with My Word, The Bible, which has been proven to be true over and over again for thousands of years.

In My Word, I gave you over 7,000 promises to help you with any problems you will face. I also left you with the gift of The Holy Spirit, who dwells in you, to help you understand My Word. If you truly want to seek Me, you will find Me as I promise in Jeremiah 29:13 – "You will seek Me and find Me when you seek Me with all your heart" *(Jeremiah 29:13, NIV)*. This will take faith which means to believe that which you cannot see.

Let Me give you an earthly example of faith. A father wants to teach his son to swim, so he tells his child to trust him and jump into his arms. The child is afraid as he knows he cannot swim. The more he hears his father say "trust Me son, I will catch you," the more he believes this to be true, so he takes a leap of faith and his father catches him. He did not put his faith in his own ability, rather in his trust that his father, who loves him, will catch him.

I, your Heavenly Father, love you much more than your earthly father so you need to trust Me. To obtain this trust, you must develop an intimate relationship with Me. By studying My Word, and all My promises, and the depth of My love for you, you will come to know Me and believe in Me.

My Spirit will be your guide in understanding My word. All you have to do is ask Him. You see I made no one quite like you! You have a purpose in life that I will reveal to you, if you truly believe. Find comfort in My promise in Jeremiah 29:11 – *"For I know the plans I have for you," declares the LORD, "plans to prosper you and not to harm you, plans to give you hope and a future" (Jeremiah 29:11, NIV)*

You were not meant to go through life on your own. I will place just the right people of faith to help you on your journey. I did not promise you days without pain, laughter and no tears, or sun without rain. What I do promise is strength for the day, comfort for the pain, and light for the way. So, if I allow something to happen in your life, I will bring you through it as nothing is impossible with Me, as I promise in Matthew 19:26 – *I (Jesus) looked at them and said, "With man this is impossible, but with God all things are possible" (Matthew 19:26, NIV).*

In developing an intimate relationship with Me, you will have a deep desire to help others. I will show you how to do this and your heart with be filled with joy! You are going to be amazed at what I will do with your life! I love you My dear child and will NEVER leave you!

Bullying

My precious child, I see you with such fear and worry over that bully that won't seem to leave you alone. This makes you feel like no one is beside you.

Let Me start by saying you are never alone. I am with you always and will never leave you.

When I walked this Earth many years ago, I, too was picked on and ridiculed so I understand what you are going through. That is why I left you with My Word, the Bible, which was meant to be your guide through life. It has over 7,000 promises that will help you through any problem. I also left you with the gift of The Holy Spirit which will help you understand My Word. All you have to do is ask Him!

Please read and find comfort in the following promise; Deuteronomy 31:6 – *"Be strong and courageous! Do not be afraid and do not panic before them. For the LORD your God will personally go ahead of you. I will neither fail you nor abandon you"* (Deuteronomy 31:6, NLT).

I knew you would face problems in this world, so My biggest message in The Bible is "do not be afraid." When you pray to Me I promise I will listen and help you. Sometimes that help is through someone else so do not try to handle this situation alone. I would never allow anything to happen to you without providing you with the strength to handle it, as I love you so much! I promised this in Psalm 18:3 – *"I called on the LORD, who is worthy of praise, and he saved Me from My enemies"* (Pslam 18:3, NLT).

For inspiration read the story of David and Goliath which is found in the Bible in 1 Samuel chapter 17. The giant Goliath was challenging God's people to stand up to him and David's faith was so strong that with God's help he was able to defeat the giant. This story shows if you trust in Me, no matter how afraid you are, I will be your strength!

Do not try to get even with a bully, let Me take care of them. You should love your neighbor as you love yourself. It is ok to hate the bully's actions - but Love them, as they are also a child of Mine. These actions come from the devil and I can handle evil.

Read My promise in Romans 12:19 – *"Do not take revenge, My dear friends, but leave room for God's wrath, for it is written: "It is mine to avenge; I will repay, says the Lord" (Romans 12:19, NIV).* This does not mean you must tolerate the situation, it simply means to seek My guidance and I will show you what to do. Remember My help may come to you from someone else, so pay attention and pray.

Sometimes it is easier to handle when you understand why people bully. Hurting people hurt, so there is something going on in their life that is causing this to happen. It may be that they too are being bullied or they have a bad situation at home. They may be doing this to get attention or they may just be jealous of you. Whatever the reason, pray for Me to help them too. By doing so that will show you love and trust Me. I will turn your pain to purpose!

Remember you are My masterpiece. There is no one quite like you! I gave you certain gifts, talents and a unique personality. Stay close to Me in prayer and I will tell you My purpose for your life. You are going to be amazed at My plans for you! I love you My dear child and will NEVER leave you!

Cancer / Chronic Diseases

My dearest child, I see you with so much worry over your recent diagnosis and that saddens Me. I did not create you to leave you all alone. I gave you My Word, The Bible to be your compass through life. It has over 7,000 promises to help you through this life.

I have great plans for you that you do not see now as stated in Jeremiah 29:11 -- *"For I know the plans I have for you declares the Lord, plans to prosper you and not to harm you, plans to give you hope and a future" (Jeremiah 29:11, NIV).*

You live in a fallen world, My child, where illnesses and trials exist. One of My many promises to you is the fact that I will never leave you as stated in Isaiah 41:10 -- *"So do not fear, for I am with you; do not be dismayed, for I am your God. I will strengthen you and help you; I will uphold you with My righteous right hand" (Isaiah 41:10, NIV).*

Do not let this disease define you. You are My child! Give this to Me and let your Faith be bigger than your fears and together we will get through this. I have placed many people in your life to help you too, so accept their help and be thankful.

This world will tell you that you need to be strong I tell you to let Me be your strength. I will never allow anything to happen to you My child without giving you what you need to endure it.

I will also turn this pain and suffering to a purpose that you will see soon.

In the meantime, turn away from worry and replace it with prayer and I will bring you peace as stated in Matthew 11:28 -- *"Come to Me, all you who are weary and burdened, and I will give you rest" (Matthew 11:28, NIV).* I see you looking at the doctor's report with much fear. Never forget the many miracles I perform daily. What is told to you by human standards may not be My will for you. When you find your mind worrying about tomorrow please find comfort in Matthew 6:34 -- *"So do not worry about tomorrow; for tomorrow will take care of itself. Each day has enough trouble of its own" (Matthew 6:34, NASB).*

Remember My promises do not change for I am the God of yesterday, today and tomorrow. I will give you enough Grace for one day at a time.

Every morning when you get up say My name and I will be there waiting to help you through the day. I did not promise days without pain, laughter and no tears, or sun without rain. What I do promise is strength for the day, comfort for the pain, and light for the way.

So, if I allow something to happen in your life, I will bring you through it. So, rest in Me, My child and I will give you peace as stated in John 14:27 - *"Peace I leave with you; My peace I give you. I do not give to you as the world gives. Do not let your hearts be troubled and do not be afraid" (John 14:27, NIV).* Most of all remember I am with you always and will never leave you. I love you My precious child.

Caregiver

My precious child, I see you with so much anxiety while caring for your loved one.

First of all, I want you to know I am with you and I will never leave you. You are doing My will and that makes Me happy. Please find comfort in My Word, The Bible, for it will bring you peace during this difficult time in your life. Ask The Holy Spirit for understanding of My Word and He will help you.

The best way to experience the peace only I can give is by praying, reading, and meditating on My Word. Find comfort in Isaiah 41:10 – *"Don't be afraid, for I am with you. Don't be discouraged, for I am your God. I will strengthen you and help you. I will hold you up with My victorious right hand"* (Isaiah, 41:10, NIV). When I walked this Earth many years ago, I came to serve - not to be served. So,

My child, you are being an imitator of Me. You will be greatly blessed for living so selflessly!

I know this is not easy but together we can handle anything. I will put the perfect people in your life to help.

Being a caregiver, you will experience feelings of both anger and fear and both are normal. Anger, asking why this happened and wondering if you will ever have a normal life again. Fear, wondering what if it gets worse and how will you deal with the medical bills.

The answers to these questions you have no control over. Give them to Me and trust Me, for I love you My child! I am the God of yesterday, today, and tomorrow so do not worry about the future for I am already there! I promise this in Matthew 6:34 -- *"So don't worry about tomorrow, for tomorrow will bring its own worries. Today's trouble is enough for today"* (Matthew 6:34, NIV). So keep doing your best and let Me do the rest! Take one day at a time as I only provide enough grace for the day.

There may come a point when, despite all the prayers for healing and the efforts of the doctors and medicine, it becomes clear that your loved one will not recover. The idea that they will not be around much longer is hard to swallow.

At this time you will have conflicting emotions. You will want the suffering to end but at the same time you do not want to lose them. This is the time that I will be very close to you as promised in Psalm 34:18 – *"The Lord is near to the brokenhearted, and saves the crushed in spirit" (Psalm 34:18, ESV).*

These are not just words My child; these are My promises to those who trust in Me. I did not create you to leave you on your own. Take this time to talk to your loved one about any fears they may have, to apologize for any wrongdoings, express your love for them, and share beautiful memories together.

This is also the time to prepare them to meet Me. It is okay to cry as I intended tears to be a release valve. This is also a time to give them permission to die so they will not linger in worry over you or others. This will bring your love one joy knowing surviving members of the family will be taken care of.

Please read them some of My promises which are designed to give them peace as to where they're going and what to expect. The following promises will comfort them:

"Come to Me, all you who are weary and burdened, and I will give you rest" (Matthew 11:28, NIV).

Jesus replied, "Truly I tell you, today you will be with Me in paradise" (Luke 23:43, NIV).

"Let not your hearts be troubled. Believe in God, believe also in Me. In My Father's house are many rooms. If it were not so, would I have told you that I go to prepare a place for you? And if I go and prepare a place for you, I will come again and will take you to myself, that where I am you may be also" (John 14:1-3, ESV).

Do not believe that your loved one cannot hear or understand what you are saying. Ask The Holy Spirit to give you the wisdom and the door of opportunity, to share My Good News, and even a person in a coma may hear the words of Scripture. Preparing your loved one to meet Me will bring you and your loved one great peace!

When the day comes that I bring your love one home to live with Me in Paradise, you will have many mixed emotions. Your first thought will be that they are at peace. The next thought will be what are you going to do in your life without them?

While you grieve, keep Me close and read My Word, and I will show you how to move on until you are with your loved one again. This world may tell you to be strong. I tell you to let Me be your strength! I have great plans for your future My child, as promised in Jeremiah 29:11 – *"For I know the plans I have for you," declares the LORD, "plans to prosper you and not to harm you, plans to give you hope and a future" (Jeremiah 29:11, NIV).* So rest in Me and I will bring you peace! I love you, My precious child and will NEVER leave you!

Chronic Pain

My precious child, I see you in so much pain and it saddens Me. You live in a fallen world in which suffering and death are a part of, and you will not fully understand why on this side of Heaven. I understand your pain as I suffered greatly to save you from your sins and to give you an inheritance to spend eternity with Me in Heaven.

When I walked this Earth many years ago, I left you with My Word, The Bible, to be your guide through life. It has over 7,000 of My promises to comfort you. I also left you with the gift of The Holy Spirit to help you understand My Word. All you have to do is ask Him! I never meant for you to handle pain with your own strength so surrender it to Me and trust Me to be your strength as promised in Psalm 71:16 – *"I walk in the strength of the Lord God. I tell everyone that you alone are just and good" (Psalm 71:17, TLB).*

If you really trust Me, I will turn your pain to purpose. When chronic pain hits you, and you offer it up to Me, your soul opens and you will experience Me at a deep profound level. When you suffer pain and allow Me to be your guide, it will produce spiritual growth and maturity at a new level that you have never experienced before. I will not allow anything in your life without giving you the strength to endure it!

By keeping Me close in prayer and studying My Word, together we will get through this. Nothing is impossible with Me.

I promised you this in Matthew 19:26 – *"Jesus looked at them and said, "With man this is impossible, but with God all things are possible" (Matthew 19:26, NIV).*

When the doctors tell you there is nothing more they can do and you have to live with the pain, I may have different plans for your life. My Word is much stronger than any pain medication given to you!

I may ask you to comfort others in their struggle with pain. Your pain is giving you compassion for others that may be in the same or similar situation. You may be a source of great hope for them!

This brings Me great joy when I see My children helping one another. I have great plans for your life as promised in Jeremiah 29:11— *"For I know the plans I have for you," declares the LORD, "plans to prosper you and not to harm you, plans to give you hope and a future" (Jeremiah 29:11, NIV).*

You see, My dear child, you can be happy and have pain at the same time. Suffering produces intimacy with Me which will bring your heart great joy. By reading the book of Job in the Bible you will see a righteous man who lost everything. His children, property and wealth, his good name, and even his health. He does cry out to God and in God's perfect timing He answers Job. The book of Job teaches us that suffering may occur for reasons that we don't understand unless or until God reveals them to us. Job kept faithful to God and he was blessed with more than He took away.

Remember My child, I did not promise you days without pain, laughter and no tears, sun without rain. I do promise strength for the day comfort for the pain and light for the way. I love you dearly, and will never leave you.

Depression

My precious child, I see you suffering with depression and feelings of hopelessness and this saddens Me, as I love you so much! I know what you are going through as I suffered greatly when I walked this Earth many years ago. You live in a fallen world where pain and suffering are very much a part of. That is why I left you with My Word, The Bible, which contains over 7,000 promises to help you.

I also left you with the gift of The Holy Spirit. He will help you understand My Word and show you how to apply it to your life. All you have to do is ask Him. There are many stories of people who were favored by My Father, who battled depression. Job, David, Abraham, to name a few. They put their trust in God the Father and He turned their pain to purpose.

When you turn to My Word, and trust Me I will help you as promised in Proverbs 12:25 – *"Anxiety in a man's heart weighs him down, but a good word makes him glad" (Proverbs 12:25, ESV)*. When you seek an intimate relationship with Me, you will believe that you can experience love amid suffering, as there are many examples of this in the Bible.

Depression can make you feel dead but still walking. It may feel terrifying as your world feels dark, heavy, and painful. Remember, I am the light of the world as stated in John 8:12 – *"Jesus spoke to the people once more and said, 'I am the light of the world. If you follow Me, you won't have to walk in darkness, because you will have the light that leads to life'" (John 8:12, NLT)*.

You see, My child, depression tells you many lies such as: you are alone, no one loves you, you will never feel better, and everyone will be better off without you. These are the lies of the devil. I love you very much and I am always with you. I never allow pain or suffering without giving you the strength to endure it! So fight those attempts of the devil with My many promises found in The Bible.

I have great plans for you My child, as found in Jeremiah 29:11 -- *"For I know the plans I have for you," declares the LORD, "plans to prosper you and not to harm you, plans to give you hope and a future" (Jeremiah 29:11, NIV).* Remember you were not meant to handle the problems of life on your own. I will put just the right people to help you through this, if you truly trust Me.

The world tells you to 'be strong', I tell you to let Me be your strength! If you really believe this, you will be amazed at what I will do in your life! I love you My child, and I will never leave you alone, as I am with you always!

Divorce or End of a Relationship

My dear child, I see you in so much pain as the relationship that you wanted to last forever is ending and your heart is breaking. I am holding you extra close now and will carry you through this difficult time in your life as promised in Romans 8:38 – *"And I am convinced that nothing can ever separate us from God's love. Neither death nor life, neither angels nor demons, neither of our fears for today nor our worries about tomorrow - not even the powers of hell can separate us from God's love"* *(Romans 8:38, NLT).*

I do not like divorce because of the pain it causes. I see you with feelings of rejection, fear, anger, and loneliness. This saddens Me as I love you so much. The most difficult is the pain of rejection as this is the pain that says that you are not good enough or you have no value. Nothing could be further from the truth as you are My child! I will help you restore your self-worth so keep Me close and trust Me.

Your relationship was either a blessing from Me, a lesson you needed to learn, or both. If your marriage can't be fixed, no matter how hard you tried, then know that it is because I closed that door as I have better plans for you!

This I promised in Jeremiah 29:11 — *"For I know the plans I have for you," declares the LORD, "plans to prosper you and not to harm you, plans to give you hope and a future" (Jeremiah 29:11, NIV).*

Fear is the hardest thing to overcome. This comes from trying to control things that you can't. When you have those feelings of fear, hand them over to Me as I am in control! This I promised to you in 1 Peter 5:7 – *"Cast all your anxiety on Him because he cares for you" (1 Peter 5:7, NLT).* I will bring you the peace you need, if you just ask. Focus on Me and feel the peace that I give you. One day at a time, one moment at a time. I will put the perfect people in your life to help you with the fear of how you are going to move on without your loved one.

The anger you may feel is learned from the fallen world that you live in. You expect everything and everyone to be perfect. What your mind perceives as perfect is not. This is why you need Me! You may be angry at many people and things that are going on around you at this time, feeling like you are in a battle of your own. Pay attention to what I said in Proverbs 14:16 -- *"A wise man is cautious and turns away from evil, but a fool is easily angered and is careless" (Proverbs 14:16, NASB)*. But know My child, I am right there with you. So focus on Me and allow My peace to calm you.

Loneliness is another void that I will fill with the right people. They will fill your days with hope if you listen to them, for this is why I sent them. Lean on them as I will be working through them. By reading My promises in The Bible and asking for guidance from The Holy Spirit to understand them, I promise time will heal your wounds and you will see My purpose for your life.

True happiness comes from a deep loving relationship with Me. I will show you the path I want you to take and you will live for Me and experience happiness and peace that this world cannot give! Do not worry about your future for I am already there. Take one day at a time as I will give you enough of My grace only for the day.

Surrender your future to Me and thank Me for showing you the depth of My love for you! You will be amazed at what I will do for you! I love you My child and will NEVER leave you!

Envy

My dear child, I see you with envy in your heart and it saddens Me. I made you unique and no one on this planet has the exact life experiences, gifts, talents, and abilities as you. I made you for a specific purpose that is yours alone. When you seek an intimate relationship with Me, I will reveal My plan for your life. To do this you must read My Word, The Bible, which I left you to be your guide through life. It contains over 7,000 promises to help you along your path in life. I also left you with My gift of The Holy Spirit, to help you understand My Word. All you have to do is ask Him!

When you are jealous of what someone else has, you are telling Me that you are not satisfied with what I have given you! I have great plans for your life as I promise in Jeremiah 29:11— *"For I know the plans I have for you," declares the LORD, "plans to prosper you and not to harm you, plans to give you hope and a future" (Jeremiah 29:11, NIV)*. To get jealousy out of your heart, you need to stop focusing on what others have and focus on Me and what I have already blessed you with. You were made to imitate Me so ask The Holy Spirit who dwells in you to show you ways to do this.

When you imitate Me, He will produce the fruits of salvation which are promised in Galatians 5:22 – "But The Holy Spirit produces this kind of fruit in our lives: love, joy, peace, patience, kindness, goodness, faithfulness" *(Galatians 5:22, NLT)*.

The only way to receive the perfect love I have for you and to discover what My plans are for you is to open your heart and follow Me. When you read My word and keep Me close to you in prayer, I will draw near to you. This I promise in James 4:8 -- *"Come close to God, and He will come close to you. Wash your hands, you sinners; purify your hearts, for your loyalty is divided between Me and the world" (James 4:8, NLT)*.

When I walked this Earth many years ago, I came to serve not to be served. To find true happiness and peace you must do the same. Ask Me every day how to serve others and your heart will be at peace. To die to yourself and live for others is very pleasing to Me. Be thankful for everything I have given you as I love a thankful heart!

You live in a fallen world where sin is very much a part of. Everyone has problems of their own. I never allow trials in your life without giving you the strength to handle them. I never promised days without pain, laughter and no tears, or sun without rain. What I do promise is, strength for the day, comfort for the pain and light for the way!

So focus on My purpose for your life. Do not compare yourself to others. I am a loving God and I know what is best for YOU. I love you My child and will NEVER leave you!

Financial Worries

My dear child, I see you with so much worry about money and how you are going to pay your bills. This saddens Me as I did not create you to worry. When I walked this Earth many years ago, I left you with My Word, The Bible and The Holy Spirit, to be your guide in life. It contains over 7,000 promises to help you through all of life's problems. I did not create you to leave you on your own as promised in Philippians 4:19 – *"And My God will meet all your needs according to the riches of his glory in Christ Jesus" (Philippians 4:19, NIV).*

There are many reasons for having money problems: 1) recent job loss 2) overspending 3) not making enough money or 4) many medical bills. These are just a few as there are many more. If the reason is in your control pray to Me for guidance and I will help you. Most money problems are out of your control but nothing is impossible with Me as stated in Matthew 19:26 -- *"Jesus looked at* them and said, *"With man this is impossible, but with God all things are possible" (Matthew 19:26, NIV).* So you see if you have faith and truly believe in your heart that I can change this situation and turn it around for your good and My Glory I will do so My child.

By reading My Word, and meditating on it, this will help you to develop an intimate relationship with Me. You will then see nothing happens that escapes Me! You will also see the deep love I have for you and know that I have great plans for your future as promised in Jeremiah 29:11 – *"For I know the plans I have for you," declares the LORD "plans to prosper you and not to harm you, plans to give you hope and a future" (Jeremiah 29:11, NIV).* You see My child, I created you with unique gifts and talents that only you have. I will reveal these to you in My way and My time. By learning to trust Me you will experience great peace while I change you from the inside.

Being patient while I work in you will be hard at times, so claim a few of My many promises as your own and you will experience the peace only I can give. If I answered your prayers all at once, you would be overwhelmed! By trusting in Me and praying to Me, you will see My plan unfold in your life. You will be amazed! So when the devil tells you it will not happen or you will always have money problems simply say My name and I will be there.

One of the greatest ways you can show Me you trust Me is by helping others. This is very pleasing to Me. When you forget about your temporary problems and reach out to help others you will blessed beyond your expectations. Get up every day and ask Me to show you ways to be a blessing to others and thank Me for the many blessings I have already given you. You will then begin to see My plan for your life. There will be many times that you will doubt as you are human and live in a fallen world. During these times ask for more faith and believe that I will provide you with it! You were meant to live one day at a time, so I will provide you with enough Grace for just one day. This builds your faith and allows you to truly trust Me.

Remember, My dear child, I am also a God of surprises so My blessings may be right around the corner. Trust in Me and surrender this to Me and watch what I do in your life. I love you, My child, and will never leave you!

Forgiveness

My precious child, I see you with so much anger, resentment and bitterness that your heart is not able to forgive. To find true peace and happiness you must be an imitator of Me. When I walked this Earth many years ago I showed you the ultimate act of forgiveness, My suffering and death on the cross. One of My last statements before I died was Luke 23:34 NLT- *I said, "Father, forgive them, for they don't know what they are doing" (Luke 23:34, NLT).* And the soldiers gambled for My clothes by throwing dice. You will learn so much about the gift of forgiveness in My Word, The Bible, which was meant to be your compass through life.

You live in a fallen world and are all sinners and deserve My judgement, but in My deep love for you I gave you the gift of forgiveness. It is very simple My child. I lavish you every day with My forgiveness so you must forgive others as I forgive you. In praying The Lord's Prayer, I make reference to forgiving others when it says "and forgive us our trespasses as we forgive those who trespass against us." This means My child I will forgive you as you forgive others.

If the other person is really sorry you must find it in your heart to forgive them. I never give up on you so never stop forgiving. If you take the sin of pride out, your heart will be open to forgive. Forgiveness may be a daily thing for something horrible that happened earlier when someone harmed you or a loved one. That person was under the devil's spell and deserves forgiveness. Keep Me close and I will bring your heart to full forgiveness so you can experience the peace and joy only I can provide.

You must also learn to forgive yourself. This may be more difficult than forgiving others as they do not live in your head. That constant voice in your head that condemns you is the voice of the devil as I would never do that to you because of the love I have for you. Go to your brother or sister with a sincere heart and ask for forgiveness and repent and then forgive yourself.

Your heart and mental health may depend on your ability to reduce hurt and anger and other self-destructive behaviors. Forgiveness is an effective tool for your well-being as it can enhance your health and relationships and even prevent diseases. My gift of forgiveness means to take less personal offense, as everyone is going through something, this will help you reduce anger which will keep your heart healthy.

When I forgave the thief on the cross next to Me his gift was eternal life with Me as I stated in Luke 23:43 -- *And I replied, "I assure you, today you will be with Me in paradise" (Luke 23:43, NLT).* So you see, My child, the benefits of forgiveness are amazing. When someone hurts you, and you forgive them, it does not mean that you have to resume a relationship with them, nor does it mean you have to forget what happened. It simply means when you remember the situation you do so with no pain just an understanding of how I helped you through it.

Forgiveness is a gift for you, you My child. A gift that allows you to move on under My constant love and protection. Keep Me close to you, and trust in Me, and I will help you through any situation where you find it difficult to forgive someone. Once you move past that difficult situation, your heart will be filled with the peace that only I can give. I promise you, My child, I love you very much and will never leave you alone to face any problem.

Grief

My precious, precious child. I see you with so much sadness over the loss of a dear loved one. I know your heart is breaking and this saddens Me. It is times like these that I carry you as I love you so much. At times the pain may feel unbearable and you will feel like you cannot go on without them. Lean on Me and I will be your strength as I promise in Isaiah 41:10 – *"Don't be afraid, for I am with you. Don't be discouraged, for I am your God. I will strengthen you and help you. I will hold you up with My victorious right hand" (Isaiah 41:10, NLT).*

I did not create you to leave you on your own for I knew the loss of a loved one would be the most difficult pain to bear. This is why I left you with My Word, the Bible which contains many promises of mine that will heal your heart and bring you the peace only I can provide. When you think of them try not to think of how they suffered rather remember how they enjoyed life to the fullest!

They are at peace with Me and have no more suffering.

Right now it most likely seems like you will never be able to get through this. You will always have an empty space in your heart for your loved one. Over time, with Me, you will learn to go on with your life to fulfill My purpose for you as I promised in Jeremiah 29:11 – *"For I know the plans I have for you," declares the LORD "plans to prosper you and not to harm you, plans to give you hope and a future" (Jeremiah 29:11, NIV).*

No one can tell you how to grieve. It is a very personal process. By developing an intimate relationship with Me, I will be your guide through this process. I created tears to be your release valve so do not hold them back. I will send the perfect people to help you so let them do what I asked of them and thank them for being there for you.

Remember, I did not create you to handle pain alone. Support groups with My children who have lost loved ones will be of great help to you. I turned their pain into purpose as I will do with you.

The world says you need to be strong, I tell you let Me be your strength! I am your rock as stated in

Psalm 18:2 – *"The LORD is my rock and my fortress and my deliverer, my God, my rock, in whom I take refuge; my shield and the horn of my salvation, my stronghold" (Psalm 18:2, ESV).*

You may be tempted to turn to worldly vices to get you through this. I tell you all you need is to turn to My promises and trust Me and I will provide your heart with the peace it so longs for. I did not take them as any kind of punishment for them or for you as I am a loving God! Also remember there was nothing you could have done, My child to prevent this from happening. When you prayed for a miracle I gave you one. My Resurrection was one of My greatest miracles! So rejoice for your loved one is happy with Me and you will be with them again in Paradise.

Keep Me close and when you have days where you feel you cannot go on simply say My name and I will help you. I will give you enough of My Grace for one day at a time so do not worry about the future as I am already there! I will show you how to live out My purpose for your life until you see them again in Heaven! I love you so much My precious child!

Searching For Purpose In Your Life

My precious child, I see you have reached a time in your life where you are searching for purpose. I created you with a unique, specific, personal purpose in this life that only you can fulfill. When I walked this Earth many years ago, I left you with My Word, The Bible, which has over 7000 promises, to guide you through life. I also provided you with the gift of The Holy Spirit, who will help you to understand My Word and how to apply it to your life. All you have to do is ask Him!

You will be amazed at My plan for your life which will bring you total happiness and peace that this world cannot provide. Find comfort in Jeremiah 29:11 – *"For I know the plans I have for you,"* declares the LORD *"plans to prosper you and not to harm you, plans to give you hope and a future"* (Jeremiah 29:11, NIV).

This world will tell you to follow the desires of your flesh, which may be a bigger house, a nicer car, an important career, social status and so on. While these are pleasures that I have provided for you to enjoy, they will only bring you temporary happiness. If you keep seeking only these things, you will always find yourself seeking for purpose in your life, as true happiness only comes from Me!

So share with Me your biggest dreams for your life. Do not be afraid to dream big for nothing is impossible with Me as promised in Matthew 19:26 -- I looked at them and said, "With man this is impossible, but with God all things are possible" *(Matthew 19:26, NIV)*. This will require faith My child! The more faith you have the more blessings I will give you. By studying My Word, and getting to know Me better you will be able to tell if your dream is from Me. Do not worry about when and how the dream will happen, for I will take care of that! Just follow Me and I will lead you every step of the way!

You live in a fallen world where evil is very real. Be prepared for the devil to try to put his thoughts in your head as he does not want you to follow Me. He will say things like: "you can't do this" or "why would God choose you?" Any thoughts that are not loving and encouraging are from the devil not your Loving, Faithful, Just God!

It pleases Me when you seek My will not what the world tells you!

You will slowly see My plan unfold in My time and this will bring your heart joy! This will not be easy and at times you may give in to earthly desires but simply say My name and I will bring you back. This will be a daily process, but fear not for I will give you enough of My Grace for one day at a time. By following Me, you will have a deep desire to help others. This is very pleasing to Me and will bring you joy!

Do not compare your life to others, as I have a different plan for each of My children. I also love a thankful heart, so do not forget to thank Me for all of your blessings.

Start each morning asking The Holy Spirit to bring meaning to My Word, and you will see the amazing, wonderful, plan I have for you!

Remember My child, I love you very much and will never leave you.

Loneliness

My dear child, I see you with feelings of loneliness and that saddens Me as I love you so much! I understand fully what you are going through that is why I made available to you My Word, The Bible, to be your compass in life. I also left you with the gift of The Holy Spirit to help you understand My Word. It contains over 7,000 of My promises to you and was meant to help you through all of life's problems. Let Me start by telling you that in times like these that I carry you, My child! You are NEVER alone for I am with you as promised in Isaiah 41:10 – *"Don't be afraid, for I am with you. Don't be discouraged, for I am your God, I will strengthen you and help you. I will hold you up with My victorious right hand" (Isaiah 41:10, NLT).*

I did not create you to live this wonderful life on your own. Loneliness is a state of mind, an emotion brought on by feelings of separation from other human beings. The feeling of loneliness is a temptation from the devil to make you feel separated from Me. Nothing could be further from the truth! How do you handle these attempts from the devil? By developing a close, intimate relationship with Me by reading My Word, and allowing My promises to bring your heart peace.

I am a loving and faithful God. If you trust Me and believe in Me I will turn your loneliness to purpose as I have great plans for your life as I promise in Jeremiah 29:11 – *"For I know the plans I have for you," declares the LORD "plans to prosper you and not to harm you, plans to give you hope and a future" (Jeremiah 29:11, NIV).* All you have to do is ask Me and I will help you develop the skills and confidence to reach out to others. I will place the perfect people in your life to help you accomplish My plans for you. This will bring your heart happiness and joy as you journey through life.

One of the most fulfilling ways to find true happiness and peace is by being a blessing to others as this is very pleasing to Me. By developing an intimate relationship with Me, your heart's desire will be to help others.

Loneliness often comes from trying to fulfill earthly desires. When your deepest desire is to live for Me you will experience the kind of peace that only I can give as promised in John 14:27 -- "*I am leaving you with a gift — peace of mind and heart.*" And the peace I give is a gift the world cannot give. So don't be troubled or afraid. I am a Master at turning pain to purpose. *(John 14:27, NLT).*

The following are reasons that I may have allowed you to experience loneliness. 1) to turn your attention to Me. 2) to develop skills to reach out to others with the same feeling. 3) to just get you to slow down in life and meditate on My Word as when your mind is too busy you cannot hear Me. I have great plans for you and in trusting Me to get you through this I will reveal these plans for you. So you see My precious child, I am always working in your life. All you have to do to experience My peace and joy is praying without ceasing, worry about nothing, reach out to others and help them, and thank Me for trials in your life. These trials allow My strength to shine and My Will to succeed. I love you My precious child, and will never leave you alone to face any of your troubles.

Loss of Job

My dear child, I see you with so much worry about being unemployed and being unable to pay your bills. First of all, I am with you and will help you through this if you trust Me. I love you and want what is best for you! I did not create you just to leave you on your own.

I gave you My Word, The Bible, to be your compass in life. It contains over 7,000 promises! I also left you with the gift of The Holy Spirit who will help you understand My Word! All you have to is ask Him! My biggest message is "do not be afraid." Things happen in this world that you may not understand. Have faith in Me and you will be amazed at what I will do in your life!

I made this promise to you in Romans 8:28 – "And we know that in all things God works for the good of those who love him, who have been called according to his purpose" *(Romans 8:28, NLT)*. I love you very much and this is not punishment for you.

Look for My blessings during this time. I may have a different path for you to take. One that will be more fulfilling. At times My blessings are not in what I give rather in what I take away. I will open new doors for you if you trust Me.

By developing an intimate relationship with Me you will see the path I want you to take. Through constant prayer and studying and meditating on My Word, I will reveal what My plan is for you. I make all of My children unique and all have special gifts and talents. Look for what you find joy in doing as that is where you will find My will for your life.

This world tells you that money and fame are most important but they will never provide you with the peace, joy, and contentment that you will have in doing My will. Search for the gifts I gave you and work on developing those to fulfill My purpose.

Many people do things they do not enjoy just to earn a living. That is not living, that is existing. I have great plans for you My child. I make this promise in Jeremiah 29:11 – *"For I know the plans I have for you," declares the LORD "plans to prosper you and not to harm you, plans to give you hope and a future" (Jeremiah 29:11, NIV).*

While you pray and trust Me, I will be working behind the scenes to line up just the right people and the right situation in the perfect time. Get up every day and work towards My purpose for you. If you get lost I will direct your steps. During this time in your life, look for ways to be a blessing to others, as this is pleasing to Me! It is amazing how it makes you feel to put others needs first and watch the wonderful things that I bless you with, for whatsoever you do for the least of My brothers you do for Me and you will be richly blessed. So My dear child everything works out for those who put their future in My loving hands!

So keep praying, stop worrying, and surrender it all to Me! Remember My child, I am with you always and will never leave you! I love you!

Suicidal Thoughts

My dear child, I see you with feelings of hopelessness, worthlessness, and despair with no end in sight. You are thinking of taking your life as the only way out. This saddens Me as I love you very much and created you for a purpose. You live in a fallen world so all will feel broken at times. When this feeling overwhelms you, give it to Me as during these times I am closest to you as I promise in Psalm 34:18 – *"I am near to the brokenhearted, and saves the crushed in spirit"* *(Psalm 34:18, ESV)*.

At these lowest times I carry you My child. I also put the right people in your life to help you. Do not keep these feelings to yourself. Talk to someone you trust and they will help you. Do you not feel ashamed to tell them as every person on this Earth has their own trials and tribulations to bear. They will understand more than you will ever know because I will ask them to help you.

Human feelings can be tied to life's circumstances which change constantly while My Word, the Bible, is certain and never changes. So ask The Holy Spirit to help you to understand My Word and you will find comfort as I promise in 1 Peter 5:7 – *"Give all your worries and cares to Me, for I care about you" (1 Peter 5:7, NLT).* My precious child, you were meant for a relationship with Me but when you go it alone you carry all burdens yourself.

Give it all to Me and in due time I will turn your pain to purpose. I have created no one quite like you and have great plans for your life as I promise in Jeremiah 29:11 – *"For I know the plans I have for you," declares the LORD "plans to prosper you and not to harm you, plans to give you hope and a future" (Jeremiah 29:11, NIV).*

It may look like there is no way out right now but believe and trust in Me and I will show you a way out. This world tells you that to be successful, you must have a lot of money, an important job, make good grades, have a lot of friends, look a certain way and so on. I tell you not to look at the things of this world to be happy as happiness comes from within, it comes from an intimate relationship with Me. Only with Me will your soul find true peace as I promise in John 14:27 -- "I am leaving you with a gift —peace of mind and heart. And the peace I give is a gift the world cannot give. So don't be troubled or afraid" *(John 14:27, NLT)*.

You will find answers to all of life's problems in The Bible. I left you with My promises knowing you live in a world of sin and you will see My biggest message is do not fear.

Keep Me close. Do not compare your life to anyone else as each person has their own trials to endure. What someone appears to have on the outside may not be what is on the inside. So let go of trying to control everything on your own and surrender your life to Me and watch what I will do. You will be amazed! When the feelings of sadness come, simply call My name and I will be your guide. For I am with you always and will never leave you.

Thankfulness

My dear child, I see you with such a thankful heart and it makes Me smile! I am glad to see you realizing the depth of My love for you. I love to shower you with My blessings as stated in James 1:17 – *"Every good thing given and every perfect gift is from above, coming down from the Father of lights, with whom there is no variation or shifting shadow" (James 1:17, NASB)*. I am a loving God so providing for you brings Me great joy.

Although you live in a fallen world it is possible to give Me thanks in all circumstances as I state in Thessalonians 5:18 -- *"Give thanks in all circumstances; for this is the will of God in Christ Jesus for you" (1 Thessalonians 5:18, NLT)*.

You can still have a thankful heart regardless of what your situation is. When you grieve, hurt, become angry or sin, you can still be thankful that I will see you through everything and turn it for your good and My glory. I do not waste pain, for I will turn it in to purpose.

When you pray, I always listen and love to grant you your heart's desire as long as it fulfills My purpose for you.

Feeling and expressing appreciation is good for your soul.

Like any wise father, I want you to learn to be thankful for all My gifts. You need to be reminded that all you have is a gift from Me. Without gratefulness, you may become self-centered and arrogant thinking you achieved everything on your own. Thankfulness keeps your heart connected to Me and will bring you great peace.

When you need to be reminded of all the things I have done for you please bring the following to mind and be thankful: My unfailing love, My Grace, My victory over the grave for you, My many past answered prayers, My promise of Heaven and many, many more. I am a good, faithful, and just God.

When you pray, always pray with a thankful heart as this is pleasing to Me. This shows Me you trust Me in all situations both good and bad. Believe in your heart My child, that nothing happens in this world that escapes Me and My plans for you. You may even wonder why I allowed some things to happen. You will know all of this one day but in the meantime just trust in Me! This takes great faith, My child. Be guided by Colossians 4:2 – "Continue steadfastly in prayer, being watchful in it with thanksgiving" *(Colossians 4:2, ESV)*. At times it may be difficult to do, especially when you are enduring trials, but remember My child that nothing is impossible for Me.

Practice the prayer of thanksgiving no matter what is going on in your life and you will experience great joy and peace that is beyond your understanding. My definition of joy is not necessarily always having to be happy it is assurance that I am in control of all the details of your life and that everything is going to be all right and your choice to praise Me in all things. So keep a thankful heart at all times and watch what I will do in your life!

You will be amazed! Being thankful when times are good is easy but being thankful in times of trouble takes great faith! It is this kind of faith that is so pleasing to Me. I love you My dear child and I am pleased to see you trusting in Me ALWAYS!

Victims of Abuse or Crime

My precious child, I see the pain you are going through and it saddens Me. You live in a fallen world in which evil is a part of. I love you and I will never leave you to handle this alone. Please find comfort in My Word, The Bible, which was meant to be a compass in your life as I promised in Isaiah 41:10 – "Fear not, for I am with you; be not dismayed, for I am your God; I will strengthen you, I will help you, I will uphold you with My righteous right hand" *(Isaiah 41:10, NIV).*

I did not create evil for I am love. When I created this world I allowed for free will as I wanted you to love me of your own free will. This also allowed sin to enter this world as many have turned from Me. I know you are looking for answers as to why this happened to you. You did nothing to deserve this! If you have faith and trust in Me during these most difficult times I will bring your heart peace.

I know this will be hard to believe but I can turn this awful situation to good. The best example of this is when My Father sent Me many years ago to live on this Earth and endure extreme suffering and death on a cross. I turned this death into your inheritance to Heaven in which you will live with Me for eternity if you are committed to following Me.

In Heaven there will be no more pain, suffering, or tears. So you see My child, I will turn this to good as I promised in Jeremiah 29:11 – *"For I know the plans I have for you," declares the LORD "plans to prosper you and not to harm you, plans to give you hope and a future" (Jeremiah 29:11, NIV).* I know this is difficult to see right now but by reading and meditating on My Word and all My promises, together we will get through this. Ask The Holy Spirit to help you to understand My Word! I never allow anything to happen to you without giving you the strength to endure it.

You were not meant to handle this on your own. I will put the right people in your life to help you. You do not have to be strong for that is My job. I am much bigger than all of this!

This is a time where you may question your faith and that is normal. I am a good, just, loving, and merciful God and I promise you I will hold your hand and help you through this. It saddens Me to see the evil in this world but please remember that I hate evil and My love will conquer it!

Focus on My peace and love that I am sending you at this moment.

Do not look for revenge for I will handle those responsible for your suffering. Find comfort in Romans 12:19 – *"Do not take revenge, My dear friends, but leave room for God's wrath, for it is written: "It is mine to avenge; I will repay," (Romans 12:19, NIV).* So surrender this to Me and keep Me close to your heart and together we will get through this. I will not waste this pain you are going through for I will turn it to purpose. I love you My precious child, and will never leave you!

Waiting For The Lord
To Answer Prayers

My precious child, I see you waiting with such hope for Me to answer your prayers! I am listening and in due time you will have the perfect answer. When I walked this Earth many years ago, I left you with My Word, The Bible to be your guide through life. It has over 7,000 of My promises that will help you with ALL of life's troubles. I also provided you with the gift of The Holy Spirit, who will help you to understand My Word. All you have to do is ask Him!

One of many promises on waiting is found in Isaiah 30:18 – *"Yet the LORD longs to be gracious to you; therefore, he will rise up to show you compassion. For the LORD is a God of justice. Blessed are all who wait for him"* (Isaiah 30:18, NIV). This does not mean to sit and do nothing! Keep moving in the way your heart tells you and I will direct your steps.

Remember I answer all prayers in My time and in My way, which will always be the better way! For comfort look at Isaiah 55:9 -- *"As the heavens are higher than the Earth, so are My ways higher than your ways and My thoughts than your thoughts"* *(Isiah 55:9, NLT)*. Most people will wait in one of two ways: 1) passively - which means you will wait and give up if it is not answered soon or 2) expectantly - which means being hopeful, believing and trusting that the answer is right around the corner.

In many cases, this waiting period serves as a time of preparation. If I answered all prayers right away you may not be ready to handle My way. You are going to be amazed at the plans I have for you. I love you My child, and want the best for you! You may find yourself in such a mess that you feel you are unable to wait one more second. Then in a way you never could imagine I move in suddenly and bless your life in ways beyond your wildest imagination. This will take great faith! By keeping Me close through prayer and by meditating on My Word, you will develop the kind of faith you need to trust in My timing.

Another way for Me to bless your life is for you to be a blessing to others. Get up every day and ask Me how to do this and I will put people in your life to bless. When you put your needs aside for a moment to help others this makes Me smile. I want you to imitate the way I lived on this Earth. I did not come to be served but to serve!

You will experience great joy and happiness and your life will be blessed beyond your expectations.

You are exactly where you are supposed to be in this life at this time. Be content with your life and wait for Me to lead you. I have great plans for your future as I promise in Jeremiah 29:11 – *"For I know the plans I have for you," declares the LORD "plans to prosper you and not to harm you, plans to give you hope and a future." (Jeremiah 29:11, NIV)*. So trust in Me for I am a loving, giving God.

So wait in expectation as I love to give you the desires of your heart! So take quiet time with Me in prayer and study My Word and I will bring your heart peace while I am working on your prayers. Remember My child, your prayers will not always be answered in your ways but My ways which are much better. I made you unique and gave you certain gifts to glorify Me. Pray for Me to reveal these to you and your heart will have the peace and happiness only I can provide. I love you so much and will NEVER leave you!

** Italics in Scripture quotations have been added by the author for emphasis.

About the Author

I was raised in the Catholic faith. I grew up with three brothers and a sister in a home directly across the street from St. Patrick's church and school in Fort Wayne, IN. We went to mass every morning before school, on Sundays and every day of obligation. We prayed before every meal, we went to confession, and we were educated in the Catholic religion.

Although this may appear to be strict, we were all about a year apart so we had the sibling rivalry, arguments, and battles between us. We were not perfect by any means but having this structure and knowing that God was watching, every one of us was willing to help those in need if asked. It gave us a good feeling.

As the circle of life continued, our great grandparents and grandparents passed. We attended their funerals and continued on with our lives "knowing" that they went to heaven.

Our children were being raised in the same faith. Looking back, I believe that we were doing it as more of a "ritual" than a full dedication to God. Our father passed in 2008. Although it was very sad it was not unexpected as he was ill.

All of the family had moved to Florida in 1982, with the exception of my two older brothers, Bob and Bill. Even though we were 1000 miles apart, we spoke often and usually were together during the holidays. Bill would like to surprise us and knock on our door unannounced as that was him. The fun guy. The outgoing, life of the party, anything for a laugh kind of guy. This got him into trouble while he was younger, but you had to laugh because you didn't know what he was going to do next.

In January of 2012, Bill was diagnosed with throat cancer. The doctors said it was a 98% cure rate with chemotherapy. Five months later, the cancer was gone. The following year in June of 2013 it had returned. This time with a vengeance. It had spread throughout his body. We were shocked! This wasn't supposed to happen! He just turned 53. The next several months were draining. He stayed down here in Florida with all of us. As his body slowly started to deteriorate we continued to pray. I prayed harder than I ever had. This was no ritual, I desperately wanted to keep my brother here. I read scripture to him on many occasions as it brought him peace. Somehow, he knew it was his time to go. He sat down with mom and told her he was not afraid, he knew where he was going and he was more concerned about her. He always cared about others. It would sadden him so much watching the fundraisers on the starving children in Ethiopia that he sent them money. He fed many homeless people off the street. He could spot them a mile away. He was in a restaurant one day and he saw one quite a ways away sitting under a bridge. He ordered two meals, one to go. When the waitress brought them, he immediately delivered the one to go to the homeless person before coming back and finishing his.

He stated before he died "my biggest regret is that I never really accomplished anything".

As his palliative care continued, I continued to read scripture to him which I could see had such a calming effect in his eyes which at times looked full of fear.

Heaven received another angel on February 16, 2014 as our Lord took Bill home. The months we all spent together in his last days were over.

Shock, anger, sadness, all took over at once, or so it seems. Really, God? Mom had to see this? I spent days on end staring at the ceiling after the funeral. Now what? He can't be gone. Anxiety set in, I was full of fear. Afraid of the future. I focused on Jesus asking for peace, after what seemed like eternity, I was calm. After many episodes, the results of peace came almost immediately.